THE ART OF SCALES

A NEW APPROACH TO MASTERING SCALES ON THE CELLO

Wells Cunningham, M.M.

BILL'S MUSIC SHELF

Visit us on the Web at www.melbay.com or billsmusicshelf.com

Design and layout by Jonathan Cunningham

Visit us on the Web at http://www.melbay.com
Email us at email@melbay.com

TABLE OF CONTENTS

INTRODUCTION

A NEW APPROACH TO LEARNING SCALES

Over the years I have tried every cello scale book in print. I discovered that while many had useful sections, no single book contained everything I needed for my students. I found that in order to give effective scale assignments, it was necessary to cut and paste pages from several different books with my instructions scribbled in the margins.

This led me to create an improvised, handwritten scale book that over time has evolved into the finished product you are now holding.

HOW IS THIS BOOK DIFFERENT?

Currently available scale books are a dizzying maze of everything from broken thirds and chromatic scales, to double and triple stops, all with various bowings to choose from. The instructor is forced to spend valuable lesson time flipping through pages in an effort to decide which scale, bowing, and rhythm pattern is appropriate for each student. With this book, I hope to save you the time and frustration I have personally experienced using other scale methods.

My principal goal with *The Art of Scales* is to provide students with the most essential scale exercises in an easy to follow step-by-step format. Each scale in this book is designed as a rigorous daily exercise that will take between 25-45 minutes to complete.

In this book, you will *not* find any of the following:
- Broken thirds, fourths and fifths
- Chromatic scales
- Sixths
- Whole tone scales
- Unisons
- Triple and quadruple stops
- Octaves and thirds in the lower positions, as follows:

I submit that all of the above techniques are acquired as students progress through the repertoire and need not be included as part of a daily scale routine.

THE SCALE

Each scale in this book is to be played using the acceleration patterns made famous by Ivan Galamian (p. 7). You will notice that I have included bowing and rhythm variations for the arpeggios, but not for the scales. This is because it is my opinion that scales are best learned using the acceleration patterns with straight eighth notes. Once students become proficient, you may wish to incorporate the scales with bowing and rhythm patterns (pp. 62-67).

THE ARPEGGIO

The practice of arpeggios familiarizes students with fingerboard geography, improves shifting, and eliminates fear of the upper registers. Arpeggios in this book should be practiced without a metronome. The speed of the arpeggio will naturally increase as students play larger numbers of notes within each bow, as indicated in the instructions. Arpeggios beginning on the C string are four octaves and those beginning on the G string are three octaves. This is due to the fact that four-octave arpeggios beginning on G or higher force students to play so high on the neck as to be impractical and often leads to rosin on the fingertips.

The purpose of applying bowing and rhythm variants to the arpeggio is twofold. Once students are able to play arpeggios with exceedingly complicated rhythms and bowings, shifting becomes second nature, thereby freeing students to concentrate instead on making music. Since the rhythm and bowing variants change from week to week, they have the added benefit of preventing scale work from becoming monotonous.

FLESCH ARPEGGIOS

The Flesch arpeggios contained on the page facing the scale and arpeggio are an excellent tool to help students become comfortable with extensive shifting. The principal benefit of the Flesch arpeggios is derived from their constantly changing intervals and shift distances.

OCTAVES

The benefit of practicing octaves extends beyond the ability to simply play octaves. Through daily octave practice, students learn to adjust the distance between the thumb and fingers as they move up and down the fingerboard. The octave routine in this book was designed to help students master every conceivable interval they will encounter in the cello literature.

FINGERED THIRDS

Fingered thirds are only encountered in a small handful of etudes and pieces. However, I find that regular practice of fingered thirds gives a level of comfort in thumb position that is difficult to obtain by other means.

TENTHS

Tenths are only encountered in the most virtuosic pieces and one can have a successful career in cello performance without ever having so much as attempted tenths. For those seeking an intense challenge, I have included an exercise through which tenths can be learned and mastered. Once conquered, tenths can be inserted into cadenzas with dramatic effect, although I must warn you... tenths are HARD!

A FINAL WORD

It was never my intention to write a scalebook. This book came about only after years of frustration and experimentation. I have no doubt this book will benefit your students as much as it has mine.

Please feel free to send any feedback or suggestions to feedback@artofcello.com.

-Wells Cunningham

ACCELERATION PATTERNS

These patterns are to be used with each scale in this book. In this example, the C major scale is accelerated. Notice that each pattern contains two beats, or two metronome "clicks" per bow with the exception of the 32nd notes (the last pattern), which contains three beats/bow.

(♩ = 40-60)

2-OCTAVE
Scales & Arpeggios

C Major Scale

C Major Arpeggio

A Minor Scale

A Minor Arpeggio

F Major Scale

F Major Arpeggio

D Minor Scale

D Minor Arpeggio

2-Octave Scales & Arpeggios

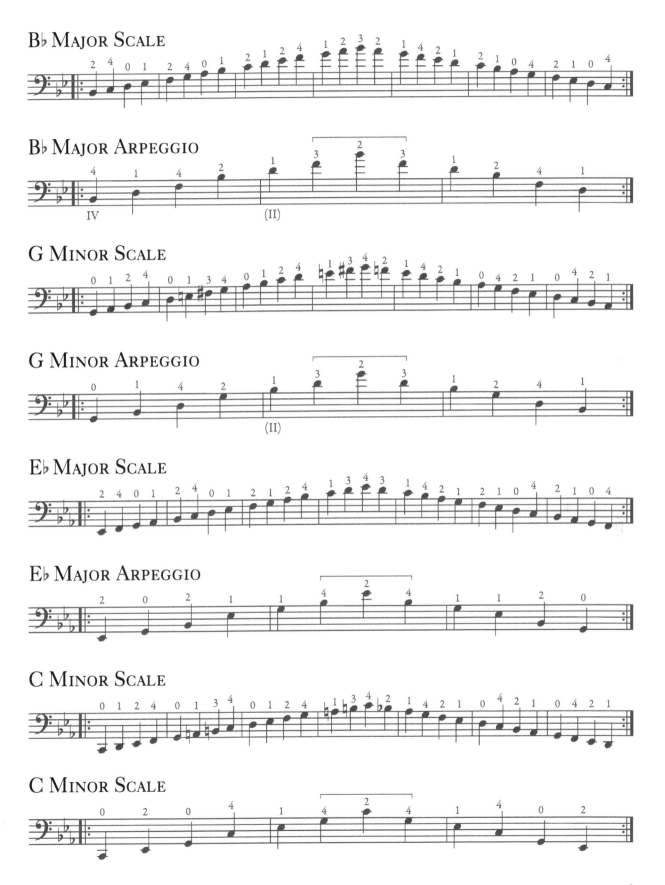

B♭ Major Scale

B♭ Major Arpeggio

G Minor Scale

G Minor Arpeggio

E♭ Major Scale

E♭ Major Arpeggio

C Minor Scale

C Minor Scale

2-Octave Scales & Arpeggios

A♭ MAJOR SCALE

A♭ MAJOR ARPEGGIO

F MINOR SCALE

F MINOR ARPEGGIO

D♭ MAJOR SCALE

D♭ MAJOR ARPEGGIO

B♭ MINOR SCALE

B♭ MINOR ARPEGGIO

2-Octave Scales & Arpeggios

F# Major Scale

F# Major Arpeggio

D# Minor Scale

D# Minor Arpeggio

B Major Scale

B Major Arpeggio

G# Minor Scale

G# Minor Arpeggio

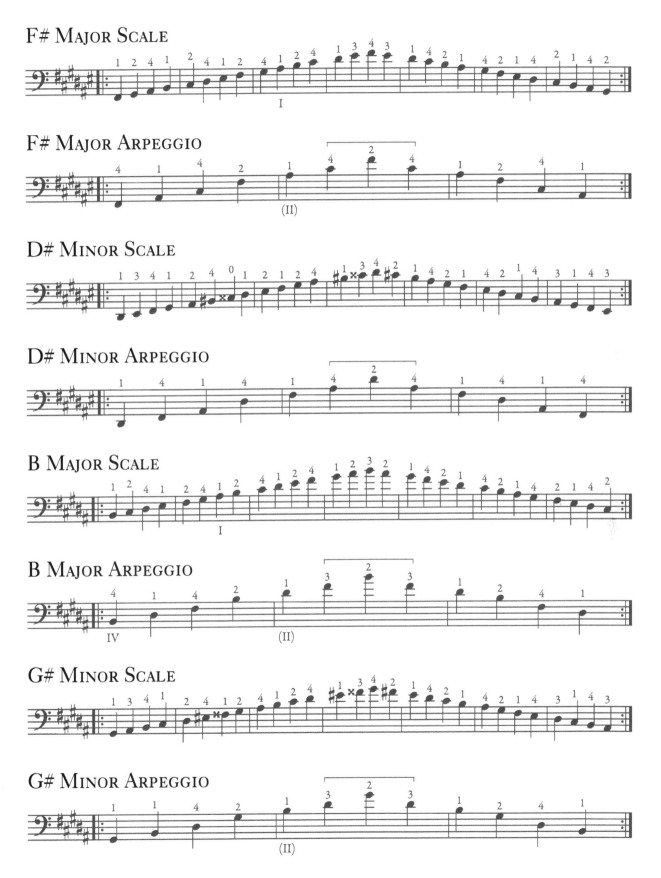

2-Octave Scales & Arpeggios

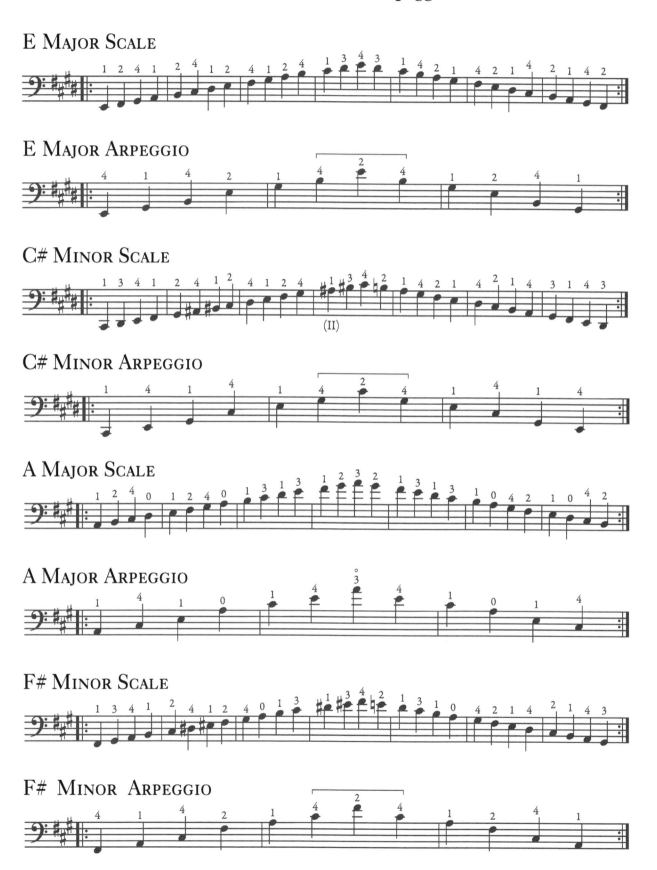

2-Octave Scales & Arpeggios

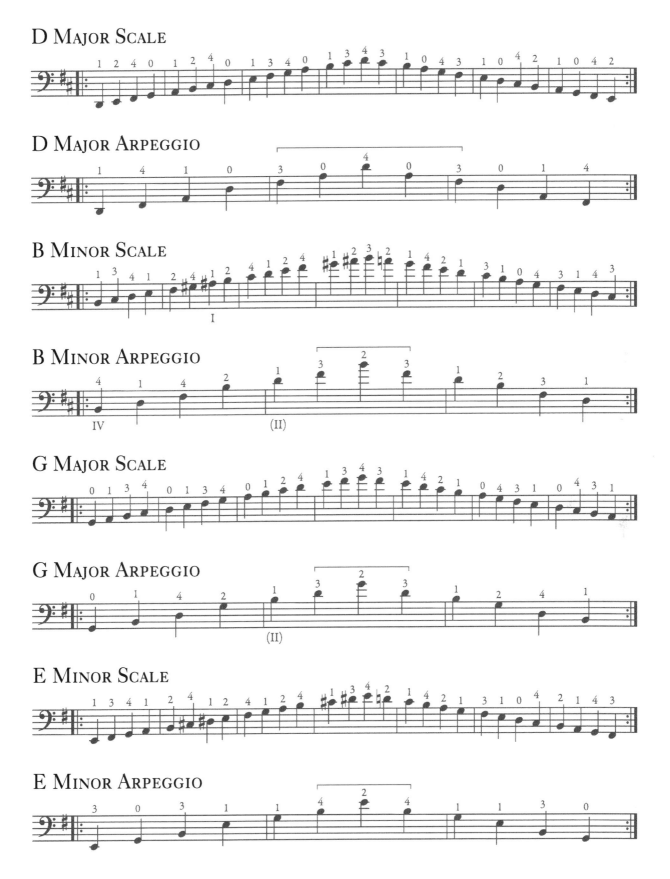

D MAJOR SCALE

D MAJOR ARPEGGIO

B MINOR SCALE

B MINOR ARPEGGIO

G MAJOR SCALE

G MAJOR ARPEGGIO

E MINOR SCALE

E MINOR ARPEGGIO

C MAJOR

SCALE
Play using acceleration patterns on page 7:

ARPEGGIO STEP 1
Play with 1, 2, then 3 notes per bow:

ARPEGGIO STEP 2
Play one of the following bowing & rhythm variants:

ARPEGGIO STEP 3
Play with 6, 12, then 24 notes per bow:

Optional Scale Work

Flesch Arpeggios

Octaves

A MINOR

SCALE
Play using acceleration patterns on page 7:

ARPEGGIO STEP 1
Play with 1, 2, then 3 notes per bow:

ARPEGGIO STEP 2
Play one of the following bowing & rhythm variants:

Beginner

Intermediate

Advanced

Virtuoso

ARPEGGIO STEP 3
Play 9 then 18 notes per bow:

Optional Scale Work

Flesch Arpeggios

Octaves

F MAJOR

SCALE
Play using acceleration patterns on page 7:

ARPEGGIO STEP 1
Play with 1, 2, then 3 notes per bow:

ARPEGGIO STEP 2
Play one of the following bowing & rhythm variants:

Beginner

Intermediate

Advanced

Virtuoso

ARPEGGIO STEP 3
Play with 6, 12, then 24 notes per bow:

FLESCH ARPEGGIOS

OCTAVES

D MINOR

SCALE
Play using acceleration patterns on page 7:

ARPEGGIO STEP 1
Play with 1, 2, then 3 notes per bow:

ARPEGGIO STEP 2
Play one of the following bowing & rhythm variants:

Beginner

Intermediate

Advanced

Virtuoso

ARPEGGIO STEP 3
Play with 6, 12, then 24 notes per bow:

Optional Scale Work

Flesch Arpeggios

Octaves

B♭ MAJOR

SCALE
Play using acceleration patterns on page 7:

ARPEGGIO STEP 1
Play with 1, 2, then 3 notes per bow:

ARPEGGIO STEP 2
Play one of the following bowing & rhythm variants:

Beginner

Intermediate

Advanced

Virtuoso

ARPEGGIO STEP 3
Play with 9 then 18 notes per bow:

Optional Scale Work

FLESCH ARPEGGIOS

OCTAVES

G MINOR

SCALE
Play using acceleration patterns on page 7:

ARPEGGIO STEP 1
Play with 1, 2, then 3 notes per bow:

ARPEGGIO STEP 2
Play one of the following bowing & rhythm variants:

Beginner

Intermediate

Advanced

Virtuoso

ARPEGGIO STEP 3
Play with 9 then 18 notes per bow:

Optional Scale Work

FLESCH ARPEGGIOS

OCTAVES

E♭ MAJOR

SCALE
Play using acceleration patterns on page 7:

ARPEGGIO STEP 1
Play with 1, 2, then 3 notes per bow:

ARPEGGIO STEP 2
Play one of the following bowing & rhythm variants:

Beginner

Intermediate

Advanced

Virtuoso

ARPEGGIO STEP 3
Play with 6, 12, then 24 notes per bow:

Optional Scale Work

FLESCH ARPEGGIOS

OCTAVES

C MINOR

SCALE
Play using acceleration patterns on page 7:

ARPEGGIO STEP I
Play with 1, 2, then 3 notes per bow:

ARPEGGIO STEP 2
Play one of the following bowing & rhythm variants:

Beginner

Intermediate

Advanced

Virtuoso

ARPEGGIO STEP 3
Play with 6, 12, then 24 notes per bow:

Optional Scale Work

Flesch Arpeggios

Octaves

A♭ MAJOR

SCALE
Play using acceleration patterns on page 7:

ARPEGGIO STEP 1
Play with 1, 2, then 3 notes per bow:

ARPEGGIO STEP 2
Play one of the following bowing & rhythm variants:

Beginner

Intermediate

Advanced

Virtuoso

ARPEGGIO STEP 3
Play with 9 then 18 notes per bow:

Optional Scale Work

FLESCH ARPEGGIOS

OCTAVES

F MINOR

SCALE
Play using acceleration patterns on page 7:

ARPEGGIO STEP I
Play with 1, 2, then 3 notes per bow:

ARPEGGIO STEP 2
Play one of the following bowing & rhythm variants:

Beginner

Intermediate

Advanced

Virtuoso

ARPEGGIO STEP 3
Play with 6, 12, then 24 notes per bow:

Optional Scale Work

Flesch Arpeggios

Octaves

D♭ MAJOR

SCALE
Play using acceleration patterns on page 7:

ARPEGGIO STEP 1
Play with 1, 2, then 3 notes per bow:

ARPEGGIO STEP 2
Play one of the following bowing & rhythm variants:

Beginner

Intermediate

Advanced

Virtuoso

ARPEGGIO STEP 3
Play with 6, 12, then 24 notes per bow:

Optional Scale Work

FLESCH ARPEGGIOS

OCTAVES

B♭ MINOR

SCALE
Play using acceleration patterns on page 7:

ARPEGGIO STEP 1
Play with 1, 2, then 3 notes per bow:

ARPEGGIO STEP 2
Play one of the following bowing & rhythm variants:

Beginner

Intermediate

Advanced

Virtuoso

ARPEGGIO STEP 3
Play with 9 then 18 notes per bow:

Optional Scale Work

FLESCH ARPEGGIOS

OCTAVES

SCALE
Play using acceleration patterns on page 7:

ARPEGGIO STEP 1
Play with 1, 2, then 3 notes per bow:

ARPEGGIO STEP 2
Play one of the following bowing & rhythm variants:

Beginner

Intermediate

Advanced

Virtuoso

ARPEGGIO STEP 3
Play with 6, 12, then 24 notes per bow:

Optional Scale Work

FLESCH ARPEGGIOS

OCTAVES

D♯ MINOR

SCALE
Play using acceleration patterns on page 7:

ARPEGGIO STEP 1
Play with 1, 2, then 3 notes per bow:

ARPEGGIO STEP 2
Play one of the following bowing & rhythm variants:

Beginner

Intermediate

Advanced

Virtuoso

ARPEGGIO STEP 3
Play with 6, 12, then 24 notes per bow:

Optional Scale Work

Flesch Arpeggios

Octaves

B MAJOR

SCALE
Play using acceleration patterns on page 7:

ARPEGGIO STEP 1
Play with 1, 2, then 3 notes per bow:

ARPEGGIO STEP 2
Play one of the following bowing & rhythm variants:

Beginner

Intermediate

Advanced

Virtuoso

ARPEGGIO STEP 3
Play with 9 then 18 notes per bow:

Optional Scale Work

FLESCH ARPEGGIOS

OCTAVES

SCALE
Play using acceleration patterns on page 7:

ARPEGGIO STEP 1
Play with 1, 2, then 3 notes per bow:

ARPEGGIO STEP 2
Play one of the following bowing & rhythm variants:

Beginner

Intermediate

Advanced

Virtuoso

ARPEGGIO STEP 3
Play with 9 then 18 notes per bow:

Optional Scale Work

FLESCH ARPEGGIOS

OCTAVES

E MAJOR

SCALE
Play using acceleration patterns on page 7:

ARPEGGIO STEP 1
Play with 1, 2, then 3 notes per bow:

ARPEGGIO STEP 2
Play one of the following bowing & rhythm variants:

Beginner

Intermediate

Advanced

Virtuoso

ARPEGGIO STEP 3
Play with 6, 12, then 24 notes per bow:

Optional Scale Work

FLESCH ARPEGGIOS

OCTAVES

C♯ MINOR

SCALE
Play using acceleration patterns on page 7:

ARPEGGIO STEP 1
Play with 1, 2, then 3 notes per bow:

ARPEGGIO STEP 2
Play one of the following bowing & rhythm variants:

Beginner

Intermediate

Advanced

Virtuoso

ARPEGGIO STEP 3
Play with 6, 12, then 24 notes per bow:

Optional Scale Work

FLESCH ARPEGGIOS

OCTAVES

A MAJOR

SCALE
Play using acceleration patterns on page 7:

ARPEGGIO STEP 1
Play with 1, 2, then 3 notes per bow:

ARPEGGIO STEP 2
Play one of the following bowing & rhythm variants:

Beginner

Intermediate

Advanced

Virtuoso

ARPEGGIO STEP 3
Play with 9 then 18 notes per bow:

Optional Scale Work

Flesch Arpeggios

Octaves

F♯ MINOR

SCALE
Play using acceleration patterns on page 7:

ARPEGGIO STEP 1
Play with 1, 2, then 3 notes per bow:

ARPEGGIO STEP 2
Play one of the following bowing & rhythm variants:

Beginner

Intermediate

Advanced

Virtuoso

ARPEGGIO STEP 3
Play with 6, 12, then 24 notes per bow:

Optional Scale Work

FLESCH ARPEGGIOS

OCTAVES

D MAJOR

SCALE
Play using acceleration patterns on page 7:

ARPEGGIO STEP 1
Play with 1, 2, then 3 notes per bow:

ARPEGGIO STEP 2
Play one of the following bowing & rhythm variants:

Beginner

Intermediate

Advanced

Virtuoso

ARPEGGIO STEP 3
Play with 6, 12, then 24 notes per bow:

Optional Scale Work

FLESCH ARPEGGIOS

OCTAVES

B MINOR

SCALE
Play using acceleration patterns on page 7:

ARPEGGIO STEP 1
Play with 1, 2, then 3 notes per bow:

ARPEGGIO STEP 2
Play one of the following bowing & rhythm variants:

Beginner

Intermediate

Advanced

Virtuoso

ARPEGGIO STEP 3
Play with 9 then 18 notes per bow:

Optional Scale Work

Flesch Arpeggios

Octaves

G MAJOR

SCALE
Play using acceleration patterns on page 7:

ARPEGGIO STEP 1
Play with 1, 2, then 3 notes per bow:

ARPEGGIO STEP 2
Play one of the following bowing & rhythm variants:

Beginner

Intermediate

Advanced

Virtuoso

ARPEGGIO STEP 3
Play with 9 then 18 notes per bow:

Optional Scale Work

Flesch Arpeggios

Octaves

E MINOR

SCALE
Play using acceleration patterns on page 7:

ARPEGGIO STEP 1
Play with 1, 2, then 3 notes per bow:

ARPEGGIO STEP 2
Play one of the following bowing & rhythm variants:

Beginner

Intermediate

Advanced

Virtuoso

ARPEGGIO STEP 3
Play with 6, 12, then 24 notes per bow:

Optional Scale Work

FLESCH ARPEGGIOS

OCTAVES

C MAJOR

A MINOR

F MAJOR

D MINOR

3-Octave Scales with Rhythm Variants

B♭ Major

G Minor

E♭ Major

C Minor

3-Octave Scales with Rhythm Variants

A♭ Flat Major

F Minor

D♭ Major

B♭ Minor

3-Octave Scales with Rhythm Variants

F# MAJOR

D# MINOR

B MAJOR

G# MINOR

3-Octave Scales with Rhythm Variants

E Major

C# Minor

A Major

F# Minor

D MAJOR

B MINOR

G MAJOR

E MINOR

ADVANCED *Studies*

C MAJOR FINGERED THIRDS

C MAJOR TENTHS

68

A Minor Fingered Thirds

A Minor Tenths

F Major Fingered Thirds

F Major Tenths

D Minor Fingered Thirds

D Minor Tenths

Bb Major Fingered Thirds

Bb Major Tenths

G MINOR FINGERED THIRDS

G MINOR TENTHS

E♭ MAJOR FINGERED THIRDS

E♭ MAJOR TENTHS

C Minor Fingered Thirds

C Minor Tenths

A♭ Major Fingered Thirds

A♭ Major Tenths

F Minor Fingered Thirds

F Minor Tenths

D♭ Major Fingered Thirds

D♭ Major Tenths

Bb Minor Fingered Thirds

Bb Minor Tenths

Advanced Studies

F# Major Fingered Thirds

F# Major Tenths

D♯ Minor Fingered Thirds

D♯ Minor Tenths

B Major Fingered Thirds

B Major Tenths

G# MINOR FINGERED THIRDS

G# MINOR TENTHS

E MAJOR FINGERED THIRDS

E MAJOR TENTHS

C♯ Minor Fingered Thirds

C♯ Minor Tenths

A Major Fingered Thirds

A Major Tenths

F# Minor Fingered Thirds

F# Minor Tenths

Advanced Studies

D Major Fingered Thirds

D Major Tenths

B MINOR FINGERED THIRDS

B MINOR TENTHS

G Major Fingered Thirds

G Major Tenths

E Minor Fingered Thirds

E Minor Tenths

NOTES

ASSIGNMENTS

DATE	SCALE	ARPEGGIO	OPTIONAL SCALEWORK
		☐ Beg ☐ Int ☐ Adv ☐ Vir	☐ Octaves ☐ Flesch ☐ Thirds ☐ Tenths
		☐ Beg ☐ Int ☐ Adv ☐ Vir	☐ Octaves ☐ Flesch ☐ Thirds ☐ Tenths
		☐ Beg ☐ Int ☐ Adv ☐ Vir	☐ Octaves ☐ Flesch ☐ Thirds ☐ Tenths
		☐ Beg ☐ Int ☐ Adv ☐ Vir	☐ Octaves ☐ Flesch ☐ Thirds ☐ Tenths
		☐ Beg ☐ Int ☐ Adv ☐ Vir	☐ Octaves ☐ Flesch ☐ Thirds ☐ Tenths
		☐ Beg ☐ Int ☐ Adv ☐ Vir	☐ Octaves ☐ Flesch ☐ Thirds ☐ Tenths
		☐ Beg ☐ Int ☐ Adv ☐ Vir	☐ Octaves ☐ Flesch ☐ Thirds ☐ Tenths
		☐ Beg ☐ Int ☐ Adv ☐ Vir	☐ Octaves ☐ Flesch ☐ Thirds ☐ Tenths
		☐ Beg ☐ Int ☐ Adv ☐ Vir	☐ Octaves ☐ Flesch ☐ Thirds ☐ Tenths
		☐ Beg ☐ Int ☐ Adv ☐ Vir	☐ Octaves ☐ Flesch ☐ Thirds ☐ Tenths
		☐ Beg ☐ Int ☐ Adv ☐ Vir	☐ Octaves ☐ Flesch ☐ Thirds ☐ Tenths
		☐ Beg ☐ Int ☐ Adv ☐ Vir	☐ Octaves ☐ Flesch ☐ Thirds ☐ Tenths
		☐ Beg ☐ Int ☐ Adv ☐ Vir	☐ Octaves ☐ Flesch ☐ Thirds ☐ Tenths
		☐ Beg ☐ Int ☐ Adv ☐ Vir	☐ Octaves ☐ Flesch ☐ Thirds ☐ Tenths
		☐ Beg ☐ Int ☐ Adv ☐ Vir	☐ Octaves ☐ Flesch ☐ Thirds ☐ Tenths
		☐ Beg ☐ Int ☐ Adv ☐ Vir	☐ Octaves ☐ Flesch ☐ Thirds ☐ Tenths
		☐ Beg ☐ Int ☐ Adv ☐ Vir	☐ Octaves ☐ Flesch ☐ Thirds ☐ Tenths
		☐ Beg ☐ Int ☐ Adv ☐ Vir	☐ Octaves ☐ Flesch ☐ Thirds ☐ Tenths
		☐ Beg ☐ Int ☐ Adv ☐ Vir	☐ Octaves ☐ Flesch ☐ Thirds ☐ Tenths
		☐ Beg ☐ Int ☐ Adv ☐ Vir	☐ Octaves ☐ Flesch ☐ Thirds ☐ Tenths
		☐ Beg ☐ Int ☐ Adv ☐ Vir	☐ Octaves ☐ Flesch ☐ Thirds ☐ Tenths
		☐ Beg ☐ Int ☐ Adv ☐ Vir	☐ Octaves ☐ Flesch ☐ Thirds ☐ Tenths
		☐ Beg ☐ Int ☐ Adv ☐ Vir	☐ Octaves ☐ Flesch ☐ Thirds ☐ Tenths
		☐ Beg ☐ Int ☐ Adv ☐ Vir	☐ Octaves ☐ Flesch ☐ Thirds ☐ Tenths
		☐ Beg ☐ Int ☐ Adv ☐ Vir	☐ Octaves ☐ Flesch ☐ Thirds ☐ Tenths
		☐ Beg ☐ Int ☐ Adv ☐ Vir	☐ Octaves ☐ Flesch ☐ Thirds ☐ Tenths
		☐ Beg ☐ Int ☐ Adv ☐ Vir	☐ Octaves ☐ Flesch ☐ Thirds ☐ Tenths
		☐ Beg ☐ Int ☐ Adv ☐ Vir	☐ Octaves ☐ Flesch ☐ Thirds ☐ Tenths
		☐ Beg ☐ Int ☐ Adv ☐ Vir	☐ Octaves ☐ Flesch ☐ Thirds ☐ Tenths
		☐ Beg ☐ Int ☐ Adv ☐ Vir	☐ Octaves ☐ Flesch ☐ Thirds ☐ Tenths
		☐ Beg ☐ Int ☐ Adv ☐ Vir	☐ Octaves ☐ Flesch ☐ Thirds ☐ Tenths

DATE	SCALE	ARPEGGIO	OPTIONAL SCALEWORK
		☐ *Beg* ☐ *Int* ☐ *Adv* ☐ *Vir*	☐ *Octaves* ☐ *Flesch* ☐ *Thirds* ☐ *Tenths*
		☐ *Beg* ☐ *Int* ☐ *Adv* ☐ *Vir*	☐ *Octaves* ☐ *Flesch* ☐ *Thirds* ☐ *Tenths*
		☐ *Beg* ☐ *Int* ☐ *Adv* ☐ *Vir*	☐ *Octaves* ☐ *Flesch* ☐ *Thirds* ☐ *Tenths*
		☐ *Beg* ☐ *Int* ☐ *Adv* ☐ *Vir*	☐ *Octaves* ☐ *Flesch* ☐ *Thirds* ☐ *Tenths*
		☐ *Beg* ☐ *Int* ☐ *Adv* ☐ *Vir*	☐ *Octaves* ☐ *Flesch* ☐ *Thirds* ☐ *Tenths*
		☐ *Beg* ☐ *Int* ☐ *Adv* ☐ *Vir*	☐ *Octaves* ☐ *Flesch* ☐ *Thirds* ☐ *Tenths*
		☐ *Beg* ☐ *Int* ☐ *Adv* ☐ *Vir*	☐ *Octaves* ☐ *Flesch* ☐ *Thirds* ☐ *Tenths*
		☐ *Beg* ☐ *Int* ☐ *Adv* ☐ *Vir*	☐ *Octaves* ☐ *Flesch* ☐ *Thirds* ☐ *Tenths*
		☐ *Beg* ☐ *Int* ☐ *Adv* ☐ *Vir*	☐ *Octaves* ☐ *Flesch* ☐ *Thirds* ☐ *Tenths*
		☐ *Beg* ☐ *Int* ☐ *Adv* ☐ *Vir*	☐ *Octaves* ☐ *Flesch* ☐ *Thirds* ☐ *Tenths*
		☐ *Beg* ☐ *Int* ☐ *Adv* ☐ *Vir*	☐ *Octaves* ☐ *Flesch* ☐ *Thirds* ☐ *Tenths*
		☐ *Beg* ☐ *Int* ☐ *Adv* ☐ *Vir*	☐ *Octaves* ☐ *Flesch* ☐ *Thirds* ☐ *Tenths*
		☐ *Beg* ☐ *Int* ☐ *Adv* ☐ *Vir*	☐ *Octaves* ☐ *Flesch* ☐ *Thirds* ☐ *Tenths*
		☐ *Beg* ☐ *Int* ☐ *Adv* ☐ *Vir*	☐ *Octaves* ☐ *Flesch* ☐ *Thirds* ☐ *Tenths*
		☐ *Beg* ☐ *Int* ☐ *Adv* ☐ *Vir*	☐ *Octaves* ☐ *Flesch* ☐ *Thirds* ☐ *Tenths*
		☐ *Beg* ☐ *Int* ☐ *Adv* ☐ *Vir*	☐ *Octaves* ☐ *Flesch* ☐ *Thirds* ☐ *Tenths*
		☐ *Beg* ☐ *Int* ☐ *Adv* ☐ *Vir*	☐ *Octaves* ☐ *Flesch* ☐ *Thirds* ☐ *Tenths*
		☐ *Beg* ☐ *Int* ☐ *Adv* ☐ *Vir*	☐ *Octaves* ☐ *Flesch* ☐ *Thirds* ☐ *Tenths*
		☐ *Beg* ☐ *Int* ☐ *Adv* ☐ *Vir*	☐ *Octaves* ☐ *Flesch* ☐ *Thirds* ☐ *Tenths*
		☐ *Beg* ☐ *Int* ☐ *Adv* ☐ *Vir*	☐ *Octaves* ☐ *Flesch* ☐ *Thirds* ☐ *Tenths*
		☐ *Beg* ☐ *Int* ☐ *Adv* ☐ *Vir*	☐ *Octaves* ☐ *Flesch* ☐ *Thirds* ☐ *Tenths*
		☐ *Beg* ☐ *Int* ☐ *Adv* ☐ *Vir*	☐ *Octaves* ☐ *Flesch* ☐ *Thirds* ☐ *Tenths*
		☐ *Beg* ☐ *Int* ☐ *Adv* ☐ *Vir*	☐ *Octaves* ☐ *Flesch* ☐ *Thirds* ☐ *Tenths*
		☐ *Beg* ☐ *Int* ☐ *Adv* ☐ *Vir*	☐ *Octaves* ☐ *Flesch* ☐ *Thirds* ☐ *Tenths*
		☐ *Beg* ☐ *Int* ☐ *Adv* ☐ *Vir*	☐ *Octaves* ☐ *Flesch* ☐ *Thirds* ☐ *Tenths*
		☐ *Beg* ☐ *Int* ☐ *Adv* ☐ *Vir*	☐ *Octaves* ☐ *Flesch* ☐ *Thirds* ☐ *Tenths*
		☐ *Beg* ☐ *Int* ☐ *Adv* ☐ *Vir*	☐ *Octaves* ☐ *Flesch* ☐ *Thirds* ☐ *Tenths*
		☐ *Beg* ☐ *Int* ☐ *Adv* ☐ *Vir*	☐ *Octaves* ☐ *Flesch* ☐ *Thirds* ☐ *Tenths*
		☐ *Beg* ☐ *Int* ☐ *Adv* ☐ *Vir*	☐ *Octaves* ☐ *Flesch* ☐ *Thirds* ☐ *Tenths*
		☐ *Beg* ☐ *Int* ☐ *Adv* ☐ *Vir*	☐ *Octaves* ☐ *Flesch* ☐ *Thirds* ☐ *Tenths*

ABOUT THE AUTHOR

Wells Cunningham received a master's degree in cello performance from the Eastman School of Music and a bachelor's degree in cello performance from the University of Miami. He is a former member of the New World Symphony and has appeared as a soloist in both the United States and Europe. Wells is currently a private teacher and studio musician in Miami, Florida.

Recordings of his playing, including the Paganini Caprice #24, can be found at www.artofcello.com.

Made in the USA
Lexington, KY
06 May 2012